dirt smudge inside cover 10/21/09

WITHDRAWN

DATE			

104

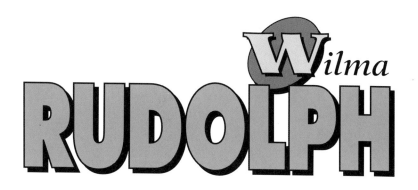

Biography

Wilma RUDOLPH

Amy Ruth

Lerner Publications Company
Minneapolis

This book is dedicated to my friend, Claire Dixon, who, like Wilma, overcame obstacles to find success and happiness. And to Judy Hoit, a writer living in Iowa City, whose life story inspires me.

Lerner Publications Company
A Division of Lerner Publishing Group
241 First Avenue North
Minneapolis, MN 55401 U.S.A.

Website address: www.lernerbooks.com

Library of Congress Cataloging-in-Publication Data

Ruth, Amy
      Wilma Rudolph / Amy Ruth.
         p.   cm. — (A&E Biography)
      Includes bibliographical references and index.
         Summary: A biography of the African-American woman who overcame crippling polio as a child to become the first woman to win three gold medals in a single Olympics.
      ISBN 0-8225-4976-X (alk. paper)
         1. Rudolph, Wilma, 1940– —Juvenile literature. 2. Runners— (Sports)—United States—Biography—Juvenile literature. [1. Rudolph, Wilma, 1940– . 2. Track and field athletes. 3. Afro-Americans— Biography. 4. Women—Biography.] I. Title. II. Series.
GV1061.15.R83R88 2000
796.42'092 — dc21
[B]   99-28291

Manufactured in the United States of America
1 2 3 4 5 6 – JR – 05 04 03 02 01 00

CONTENTS

Soon after Wilma was born, her family moved to Clarksville, Tennessee. When Wilma was growing up, Clarksville was one of many southern towns where segregation legally separated black and white citizens.

Chapter **ONE**

WILMA

WILMA RUDOLPH SAT ON HER BED, HER SKINNY
legs stretched out in front of her. As she gazed into
the air—daydreaming as usual—an older brother mas-
saged her crooked right leg, which had been partially
paralyzed by polio. His hands rubbed along the bone
and the muscles of Wilma's calf, just as his mother
had taught him. Sometimes the massages and leg ex-
ercises hurt, but Wilma didn't complain or cry out.
She knew they meant she might someday join her siblings and their friends on the playground. That was
something she wanted more than anything, because
Wilma could barely walk.

The solid determination and courage Wilma showed
during her years of painful therapy did pay off.

Wilma eventually made it to the playground, and she went on to make sports history. At the 1960 Olympic Games in Rome, Italy, sprinter Wilma Rudolph became the first American woman to win three gold medals at a single Olympics, a feat that would not be repeated for twenty-eight years.

"*I can't* are two words that have never been in my vocabulary," Wilma Rudolph once told a magazine reporter. "I believe in me more than anything in this world."

Born on June 23, 1940, in St. Bethlehem, Tennessee, Wilma Glodean Rudolph was not expected to live. She arrived two months early and weighed only four and a half pounds. Her parents, Blanche and Ed Rudolph, prayed for their tiny daughter's survival. In the 1940s, premature babies like Wilma often did not live more than a few days. Miraculously, baby Wilma began to thrive.

Ed Rudolph worked as a porter and handyman while Blanche Rudolph worked as a maid and cook and also took in sewing and laundry. During the lean years of the Great Depression (from 1929 to approximately 1942), when millions of Americans were unemployed, the family managed to scrape by without government assistance—a source of pride for Mr. and Mrs. Rudolph. The Rudolphs were devout Baptists who raised their children to cherish God, to respect and obey their elders, and to live a moral life.

The Rudolphs had a traditional marriage for the

times, in the sense that Mr. Rudolph made the rules and the decisions. "My father was a very strict man around the house; he was a disciplinarian, and he ruled with an iron hand," Wilma remembered. "When my father got home, everybody was quiet."

Wilma loved her parents very much but was somewhat in awe of her mother. "She was so proud, so strong, so religious, that I didn't think I could open up to her the way I would have liked to," Wilma remembered.

While the Rudolphs had a total of nineteen children—eleven from Ed Rudolph's first marriage and eight from his marriage with Blanche—many had grown up, moved out, and started families of their own before Wilma was born. During much of Wilma's childhood, she shared her home with six siblings—including two younger siblings.

Soon after Wilma was born, the Rudolphs moved to Clarksville, a town about twenty miles from St. Bethlehem. In Clarksville, they rented a red, wood-frame house, located in the black section of town, on Kellogg Street. The town's black citizens lived in cramped, rickety houses with no running water or electricity. The Rudolphs and other black families heated their homes by burning wood in fireplaces, and they lit kerosene lamps to see at night. Instead of an indoor bathroom, the Rudolphs used an outhouse. On the other side of Clarksville, white citizens lived in solid brick houses with modern conveniences such as indoor plumbing.

RACISM AND SEGREGATION IN THE DEEP SOUTH

Clarksville was a segregated community in the 1940s, much like other southern towns and cities. Although black people's rights were restricted throughout the South, Wilma Rudolph described race relations in Clarksville as good, because people "knew their place." Throughout the rural and urban South, black people were paid low wages to work in agricultural or service jobs. With their low wages, blacks could seldom afford to own property. Only housing in certain parts of their communities were within their means, and even then they were usually at the mercy of white landlords.

A political system known as Jim Crow treated blacks as second-class citizens for almost a century after the Civil War, which had ended in 1865. The Thirteenth, Fourteenth, and Fifteenth Amendments to the U.S. Constitution gave blacks equal rights with whites, but local governments ignored these amendments.

Southern lawmakers worked hard to prevent blacks from voting. They believed if blacks voted, they might elect black or sympathetic politicians who could take power away from whites. Local governments established expensive poll taxes to prevent blacks from voting. They also required blacks to pass literacy tests to vote. In the 1940s and 1950s, many blacks in the South did not complete junior high and high school. Financial circumstances forced them to work full time. Without proper education, they could not pass the literacy tests.

Black schools were underfunded, and teachers were underpaid. On average, a white school received twice as much money as a black school, and white teachers earned as much as one-third more than black teachers for doing the same job.

The U.S. Supreme Court decided in an 1896 case, *Plessy v. Ferguson*, that black citizens must be provided separate-but-equal public facilities. Southern states did not follow this law.

In the era of Jim Crow, blacks had to use separate public rest rooms that were rarely cleaned and were often out of order. They were prohibited, by law, from drinking from fountains marked "for whites only." On trains, blacks rode in baggage cars. On buses, they sat in the back or stood when the bus was full.

Jim Crow was also marked by violence. Members of the Ku Klux Klan, a white supremacist organization established after the Civil War, terrorized blacks by burning their homes or lynching black men for such "crimes" as looking at white women. It wasn't until the 1950s that things began to change. When Wilma Rudolph was in high school, the U.S. Supreme Court ruled in the landmark case *Brown v. Board of Education of Topeka* that segregated black schools were not equal to white schools. The Supreme Court decision effectively outlawed segregation. Southern states ignored the new ruling for several years until the federal government began enforcing it in 1958.

Inspired by civil rights leader Martin Luther King Jr., blacks organized non-violent marches and boycotts to financially hurt white business owners. As a result, blacks endured even more violence. Some whites felt their place in society was threatened by black advancement. The more radical of these whites bombed black churches, killing innocent people. Mobs of angry whites murdered black activists and were found not guilty by juries of white citizens. Police officers sprayed peaceful black demonstrators with fire hoses and turned attack dogs loose on crowds of black schoolchildren.

Black college students and other youths organized sit-ins at whites-only lunch counters and were involved in other peaceful protests to demonstrate their rights under antisegregation laws. Protesters throughout the South—including schoolchildren—were often beaten and taken to jail. Well into the 1960s, blacks and whites marched and protested to secure rights for blacks.

In 1964 the Civil Rights Act was passed. The following year, Congress passed the Voting Rights Act. Hatred and violence continued, but the federal government stepped in to assist black citizens in their efforts to receive fair and equal treatment under the nation's laws. Thousands of ordinary citizens—parents, college students, children, ministers, and many others—lost their lives in the struggle to end racism and segregation in the United States.

Only white people could attend many of the social events, such as the county fair, in Clarksville. Blacks weren't allowed inside. Wilma and other black children sat on a hill across from the fairground's main entrance, watching the whites wander in to enjoy a fun-filled day looking at exhibits, sampling fair food, and playing carnival games.

Already aware of the differences between how blacks and many whites lived, Wilma slowly began to realize just how poorly blacks were treated in Clarksville. As she watched white men groom their horses for the fair exhibits, she arrived at a startling realization. "White people treat their horses better than they treated us black people," she thought.

Signs banning blacks from restaurants and businesses were common throughout Clarksville and the South when Wilma was growing up.

At home Wilma watched her mother take care of the family, then set off to cook and clean for white families. Mrs. Rudolph worked as a maid, often delivering breakfast in bed to her employers. "The way my mother worked, somebody should have been serving her coffee in bed on Saturday mornings," Wilma wrote in her autobiography.

Wilma's lively and inquisitive personality led her to question what she saw happening in the world around her. She asked her parents why they could only find jobs serving white people, why the family could eat in only one of Clarksville's several restaurants, and why the black school wasn't nearly as good as the white one. "Never you mind" or "hold your tongue," her parents would answer. "A lot of us black kids were raised that way down South, accepting things that weren't right," Wilma wrote in her autobiography. Six-year-old Wilma decided her life would be different. She vowed to break out of the poverty and servitude that had plagued her family for generations. "I would tell myself, 'I don't know yet what the escape is going to be, but Wilma, it's not going to be like this forever.'"

Six-year-old Wilma Rudolph, right, *poses with her sister Yvonne, left.*

Chapter **TWO**

"Just Fight this Thing"

WILMA'S BATTLES DIDN'T STOP WITH DISCRIMINATION.
She was a sickly child who caught all sorts of illnesses
and had difficulty recovering. Her mother, who had
cared for many children before Wilma, used home
remedies to cure colds and coughs. Even if the family
could afford to see a doctor, there was only one black
doctor, Dr. Coleman, for the town's entire black popu-
lation. The Rudolphs called him only in cases of
emergency. Mrs. Rudolph nursed Wilma with hot
drinks and wrapped her in thick blankets to make her
sweat out the impurities that caused colds and other
illnesses.

When Wilma was four, she became gravely ill with
double pneumonia and scarlet fever. When she finally

recovered, there was still something wrong. Her right leg was crooked and partially paralyzed. Wilma had contracted polio. Doctors predicted she would never walk again. For two years, Wilma struggled to put one foot in front of the other. She had to drag herself because it hurt too much to have her weight bear down on her foot.

After the polio diagnosis, the Rudolphs took Wilma to Meharry Medical College in Nashville, Tennessee, for treatment. The Rudolphs could not afford the daily treatments recommended by the doctors or the bus fare to and from the hospital. Mrs. Rudolph, a determined and strong-willed woman, found another way. She asked the doctors to show her how to massage and exercise her daughter's leg. At least four times a day, without fail, she or one of Wilma's siblings would work Wilma's leg—massaging it and wrapping it with steaming hot towels. Once or twice a week, Wilma and her mother took the forty-five-mile trip to Nashville, where Wilma soaked her leg in a hot whirlpool bath and received other treatments in the hospital. Sometimes Dr. Coleman checked in on Wilma at her Clarksville home and offered a generous dose of encouragement. Wilma recalled the visits later: "He would say, 'Wilma, everything is gonna turn out all right. You just fight this thing, you understand?'"

In the first few years of treatment, Wilma's leg showed almost no improvement. She could barely walk, and she continued to experience pain. But the

Rudolphs refused to give up. They were determined to give their daughter every chance to become healthy. The Rudolphs believed Wilma would walk again.

When Wilma was six, the doctors in Nashville fitted her with a metal brace for her right leg. The brace attached to a sturdy brown oxford shoe that Wilma came to hate, but it did help her move around better.

Nashville was an hour bus ride from Clarksville, and Wilma and her mother—along with other black riders—had to sit at the back of the bus. When the bus was especially crowded, black people had to give up their seats for whites and stand up for the whole ride home. Wilma's treatments were exhausting and sometimes painful; usually she slept most of the way home. But on the ride to Nashville, she was enchanted with the scenery. The bus rumbled through affluent neighborhoods and past farms, pretty country houses, well-kept gardens, and white picket fences. Wilma learned about the people and communities outside of Clarksville on those long bus trips, and she imagined that someday she would live in a big beautiful house.

"[The bus rides] added a dimension to my life that the other kids didn't have," Wilma wrote in her autobiography. "I was getting out of Clarksville, I was seeing other things. I was traveling."

Until Wilma could walk on her own, the school would not allow her to enroll. While her brothers and sisters tromped off to school, Wilma took her lessons at home with a tutor. She imagined how her life would be if she could walk and run. "There really wasn't much to do but dream," Wilma said. "So I would sit around and dream about what the rest of the world was like."

Besides school Wilma missed out on other things, such as playing basketball with the neighborhood kids. Unable to participate, she did the next best thing: She watched as they darted around the court, shooting their ball at a homemade basket. Wilma, always alert, studied their moves and techniques. Sometimes the kids teased her, making fun of her crooked leg and the brace that helped her walk. As they were taunting her, Wilma vowed that someday she would show them what she was made of.

"I guess I have forgiven them, but you never really forget," Wilma told a newspaper reporter years later.

Sometimes, Wilma took the brace off secretly and tried to teach herself to walk. "I spent most of my time trying to figure out how to get my leg braces off," she said. Other times she faked a no-limp walk, desperate to be like everyone else. "[The brace] always reminded me that something was wrong with me," Wilma said. "Psychologically, wearing that brace was devastating."

At home, with six or seven siblings living in the house at any given time, there were many chores to do. Because of her disability, Wilma was excused from household work. But because she was isolated from activity in so many other ways, Wilma desperately wanted to be a part of family life. She hopped around her siblings while they completed their chores, asking questions, cracking jokes, and entertaining them any way she could. "I felt I really did have a little role, and that was to keep the rest of them going," she wrote in her autobiography. "I was like a gimpy-legged cheerleader."

Wilma learned early on about teamwork. She watched her parents struggle to support a large family in hard times, and she benefited from the love and support of her siblings who worked together to heal her leg. Together, the Rudolphs combined their strengths and skills against poverty, discrimination, and illness. "With all the love and care my family gave me, I couldn't help but get better," Wilma wrote.

Although Wilma tried to be cheerful for her family, she was sad and despondent inside. When her parents were at work and her brothers and sisters were at school, Wilma sometimes experienced grave feelings of despair. "Being left behind had a terrible effect on me," she wrote. "I was so lonely, and I felt rejected. I would just drift off into a sinking feeling, going down, down, down. I cried a lot."

When Wilma was almost eight, she was strong enough to walk on her own, with only the brace for support. Finally, she could start school. "School turned my life around," she said. "I went from being a sickly kid the other kids teased to a normal person accepted by her peer group. I needed to belong, and I finally did."

POLIO, A CRIPPLING DISEASE

Polio swept through the United States between 1890 and the 1950s, affecting tens of thousands of Americans each year. As the disease spread across the country, it raged in one region before breaking out in another part of the country. Around the time Wilma contracted the polio virus, it was most severe in the states along the Atlantic seaboard. It moved slowly westward, through Tennessee and into the Midwest.

Poliomyelitis (polio) is a virus that attacks a person's muscles and central nervous system. In the United States, the virus was most prevalent in the 1940s and 1950s, and it was often as mild as it was fatal. The disease often led to paralysis and crippling of the limbs.

When it struck in the lungs, patients needed machines called iron lungs to help them breathe. Paralysis or the collapse of vital internal muscles, such as the abdomen or throat muscles, prevented patients from eating and breathing and often led to a slow and painful death. Because it most often struck children, the virus was sometimes called infantile paralysis.

While this centuries-old disease, which dates to at least 1500 B.C., killed and crippled children for many generations, it wasn't until the late nineteenth century that it was identified and studied. The first reported epidemic began in Sweden in 1887 and swept across the world, infecting millions of people for the next seventy years.

Because the virus spread quickly among children, many parents kept their children away from public places, including swimming pools and even school. But such measures did not prevent the spread of the virus from one family member to another. In the 1940s, more children in the United States died from polio than from any other contagious disease.

While mostly affecting children, polio took other victims as well. As the epidemics continued, teenagers and adults came down with the disease. President Franklin D. Roosevelt had contracted polio in 1921 at the age of thirty-nine. For the rest of his life, he was partially paralyzed from the waist down and unable to walk unaided. He wore braces on his legs to help himself get around and often used a wheelchair. While four-year-old Wilma struggled with the onset of the disease in 1944, President Roosevelt was running the country despite his struggles because of polio. His family and staff, as well as journalists, kept his disability a secret, and many Americans didn't realize that the president of the United States could not walk on his own and needed help getting dressed and undressed.

Treatment centers, specifically for the care of polio patients, opened around the country. Doctors and nurses in regular hospitals received special training in physical therapy and warm-water treatments. Polio patients learned to walk anew with canes and braces, or they learned how to live life from wheelchairs.

Vaccines were developed in the 1950s—a decade too late to help Wilma and others like her. But thanks to the research of scientists such as Albert Sabin and Jonas Salk, who each developed separate vaccines, the deadly and crippling polio epidemics were brought to a halt. By 1957 reported polio cases dropped by eighty percent. Polio still infects some people, although there have been no reported cases in the United States since 1979. New cases of polio are rare, but 1.4 million Americans who survived polio during the epidemics still struggle with the effects of the disease.

President Roosevelt, right, *struggled with the paralysis brought on by polio throughout his presidency and much of his adult life.*

At Cobb School, Clarksville's black school, Wilma made friends and adapted to learning in a group. She soon found she couldn't daydream during school, so she slowly put the habit behind her. As she grew older, her old daydreams became her goals.

After almost three years of wearing her leg brace, Wilma decided to go out in public without it for the first time. "I'm strong enough," she thought to herself. Her weeks of practicing without the brace had given her confidence. One Sunday morning, Wilma lingered in the church parking lot before services, letting her family go in without her. Then she carefully removed the brace and walked into the church, down the aisle to her seat. Friends and neighbors strained to see Wilma, whom they knew as the sickliest girl in Clarksville, walking on her own. "From that day on, people were going to start separating me from that brace and thinking about me differently," Wilma wrote.

The church parishioners were a reliable support system in Wilma's life, much like her own family was. In general, church was important in black communities across the nation. Besides serving as a social gathering place, churches offered a haven from prejudice and discrimination. Churchgoers turned to fellow parishioners for strength in difficult times, much as Wilma and her family did.

Wilma's leg would need another two years to heal completely. Then one day when Wilma was twelve, she and her parents decided she no longer needed the brace. She had worn it less and less since that day in church. She could go on without it. With Wilma watching, Mrs. Rudolph wrapped up the brace and mailed it back to the hospital in Nashville. One evening not long after, Mr. Rudolph came home with a present for Wilma. She unwrapped the box to find a pair of black patent leather shoes, the first she had ever owned.

Once Wilma discarded the bulky brace and ugly brown oxfords for good, her life suddenly sped up. She had a lot of time to make up for, and she embraced her newfound freedom with the energy that had gone unused for almost twelve years.

"I was challenging every boy in our neighborhood at running, jumping, everything," she remembered in 1989. "I could beat most of them. I wanted to show that there was something special inside me."

Wilma fell in love with running while attending Clarksville's Burt High School. This aerial photograph shows her high school and the track field next to it.

Chapter **THREE**

SKEETER

THE SUMMER BEFORE **WILMA** ENTERED SEVENTH GRADE at the newly constructed Burt High School in Clarksville, she spent most of her time doing one thing: playing basketball. She had fallen in love with the game years earlier when all she could do was watch the neighborhood kids play. In the summer of 1952, though, Wilma and her sister Yvonne hung out in the parks shooting baskets with other kids. Wilma practiced everything she had learned about dribbling, passing, and shooting.

"It was basketball, basketball, basketball," Blanche Rudolph remembered years later. "Whenever I'd call her in to eat or to clean up, she'd be outside having a big time."

Wilma's intense interest in athletics worried her mother, who was afraid that Wilma would injure her leg on the basketball court. Mrs. Rudolph wanted Wilma to rest and play quietly indoors. But when her mother was at work, there was nothing to keep Wilma off the basketball courts. She played all day long. Wilma remembered that one of the few arguments her parents had was about her participation in basketball. In the end, Wilma's father persuaded her mother to let her play. "My father had a deep insight into the things that I wanted to accomplish as a little girl," Wilma said.

High school marked the beginning of young adulthood for Wilma. She was blossoming into a beautiful young woman with sparkling eyes and a warm friendly smile. She kept her brown hair cropped short in a style that was easy to manage and conducive to athletics. And she was growing tall. One boy in particular noticed Wilma. His name was Robert Eldridge, and he threw rocks at her to express his affection. Wilma noticed Robert too, and she decided she liked him. But Robert couldn't compete with Wilma's first love—basketball. "I wasn't obsessed with boys the way a lot of girls were," Wilma wrote. "I was more obsessed with basketball and with improving my game."

In the segregated community, school was a major social event for black youth. Wilma and her classmates hated to miss even one day of school, because that would mean missing out on social activities, gossip, and hanging out with friends. Even so, most of the students wouldn't graduate. The year Wilma enrolled in high school, only sixteen percent of black students graduated, compared with forty-three percent of white students. For poor families in the 1950s, school was a luxury. Young adults—both black and white—dropped out of school to find jobs to support their families. Girls worked as domestics—as Wilma's mother did—and boys found work in the tobacco fields, picking the tobacco crop for white farmers and landowners.

Most blacks in Clarksville, isolated by poverty, discrimination, and segregation, didn't know much about the world outside their small town. Even Wilma, with her travels to and from Nashville, knew little of the world. In 1952 twelve-year-old Wilma didn't know who was president of the United States, had never heard of the Olympics, and knew of no famous black role models to admire. Although Clarksville had been home to a few famous African Americans, including tenor Roland Hayes and violinist Clarence Cameron White, both of whom lived in Clarksville in the late 1800s, Wilma hadn't heard of either of them.

Seventh grade was an important time in Wilma's life. Her new school had a girls' basketball team, and she decided that not only would she make the team, she would excel. Determined to succeed, she asked herself, "What does it take to be the best? How long do you have to work toward being the best? What do you have to believe?" Wilma knew she had to challenge herself physically and mentally to reach her goals.

During basketball tryouts, Coach Clinton Gray decided he wanted Wilma's older sister Yvonne to be on the new team. He visited the Rudolph home and told Mr. Rudolph, who was in his sixties, that he could make Yvonne a star. Mr. Rudolph told Coach Gray that Yvonne and Wilma were a package deal. "If Yvonne is on the basketball team, then Wilma is on your basketball team also," he said. Coach Gray agreed to Mr. Rudolph's terms. Coach Gray was a kind but strict and sometimes gruff man. Although he often yelled at his players, he cared about them.

Roland Hayes, a famous African-American tenor, lived in Clarksville in the late 1800s.

If practices lasted until after dark, he drove each player home. He required all his athletes to maintain a B average in school.

Wilma was overjoyed to be on the team, even though she wasn't too pleased with the way she had landed her spot. She arrived early for every practice. "I would wear my gym clothes every day beneath my street clothes so that I could be the first person in the gym," Wilma said.

Enthusiasm and energy weren't enough to get Wilma off the bench and onto the court. For the first season—her entire seventh-grade year—Wilma was a benchwarmer. She never played in a game, but instead sat on the bench while the other players hustled on the court. Many times, Coach Gray told her not to bother dressing in her uniform for games. Coach Gray had kept his word to Mr. Rudolph: Wilma was on the basketball team. But their agreement hadn't included playing time. Another person may have sulked or pouted, but Wilma, used to waiting for what she wanted, turned a potentially negative situation into a positive one. "I did nothing but watch and study everything that was going on on the court," she wrote in her autobiography. "I watched how the rebounders positioned themselves; I studied the rules of the game and how the referees enforced them."

By the time Wilma entered eighth grade, she had the game of basketball down. She knew how to pass, dribble, rebound, shoot, and play defense. She had even

developed the timing for stealing the ball from an opponent. But still Coach Gray ignored her most of the
time. While she demonstrated grace and natural ability during hours of practice, she rarely played in
games—and then for only a few minutes at a time.

Wilma was so persistent in pestering Coach Gray to
let her play that he gave her the nickname Skeeter, because she was always buzzing around him like a mos-
quito. "You are a 'skeeter' all right," her coach teased
her. "You're little, you're fast, and you're always getting in my way."

In the spring of 1954, Coach Gray started a girls'
track team. Wilma knew that without Coach Gray's
support, she would not play on the basketball team.
Here was another way to impress him. She was one of
the first to sign up for the track team. Although he
was a fine teacher and basketball coach, Coach Gray
had no track training. He had the girls jog for an hour
after school. When the weather was poor, he had
them run down the long corridors in the school.

"Running was pure enjoyment for me," Wilma wrote
in her autobiography. "I loved the feeling of freedom
in running, the fresh air, the feeling that the only person I was really competing against was me."

Although she had to maintain a B average to stay on
the track and basketball teams, Wilma couldn't resist
the temptation to cut school with a fellow runner and
slip across the street to the municipal stadium to
practice running. When college or club track teams

were practicing there, Wilma hung around the coaches, hoping to pick up pointers. "I was more serious about track now," Wilma wrote, "thinking deep down inside me that maybe I had a future in the sport if I tried hard enough."

During track season, Coach Gray organized informal "playdays," which were like meets with other schools. Everyone who took part was recognized in some way. Wilma remembered that the focus at these events was not competition, but fun. Soon, however, a trend emerged—Wilma won every race she entered.

"I was winning without really working," Wilma remembered. "I was doing it all on natural ability... I had no idea about the technical aspects of the sport or even about all the work involved in it."

Wilma's success in track caused Coach Gray to take a second look at her. At the beginning of the basketball season in 1955, Coach Gray chose five-foot-eleven, fifteen-year-old Wilma—now a tenth grader—as one of the players to start the first game of the season. "I was the happiest person in the whole state of Tennessee," she said. The Burt High School girls' basketball team won the Middle East Tennessee Conference title that year, with Wilma leading the way to victory. In one game alone she scored 50 points. The team went on to play in the Tennessee High School Negro Girls' Championships, the state competition held in Nashville. Wilma was the star of the tournament. The girls' hard work was not enough to win the state title, however, and Wilma and her teammates experienced a disappointing loss in the finals. Despite the loss, Wilma set a school record that year, scoring 803 points over twenty-five games.

Things were going well for Wilma. Three years after discarding her detested leg brace, she was a track and basketball star at Burt High School. In its coverage of high school sports, the local newspaper often mentioned Wilma. "Wilma Rudolph continued her sensational scoring pace," wrote a reporter covering a March 1956 basketball game. The next month, the newspaper reported that "Wilma Rudolph was the big reason why the Burt Lassies [track team] won their chance to appear in the state [meet]."

Wilma enjoyed the music of Chuck Berry, a popular performer of the 1950s and 1960s.

Wilma was enjoying her time outside of athletic competition as well. She had started dating the boy who once threw rocks at her. She and Robert Eldridge, a star on the boys' basketball and football teams, were developing deep feelings for each other.

Wilma had a strong, loving, and supportive family and special girlfriends. She and her friends attended school dances, moving to the music of rock-and-roll stars like Chuck Berry and Little Richard. Wilma's best friend of all, a girl named Nancy Bowen, was also on the basketball team. Wilma's and Nancy's love for basketball made them practically inseparable. While Wilma pestered Coach Gray for more playing time, Nancy was at her side.

Despite Wilma's success on the basketball court, she was beginning to realize something important about herself and her athletic ability. "I said to myself, 'You take running seriously, and you might be a star at something yet.'"

Wilma's victories on the basketball court and the track field made her a star at Burt High School.

Chapter **FOUR**

THE ROAD
TO VICTORY

DURING THE SPRING OF 1956—WILMA'S SOPHOMORE
year in high school—she and other runners from Burt
High School traveled with Coach Gray to an important track meet at the Tuskegee Institute in Tuskegee,
Alabama. Tuskegee, an all-black university organized
in 1881 as a trade school for young black people, had
been one of the few institutions of higher education
for blacks in the nineteenth century.

Black schools from around the South entered their
girls' track teams in the Tuskegee meet, and Burt High
School faced some top-notch competition. The track
program in the Atlanta, Georgia, public schools was
particularly well known, and Coach Gray was worried
about its ability. On the drive down to Alabama, he

tried to warn the girls that they might not be as competitive as they thought. Running against some of the
best athletes in the South would be different from
running in the playdays at home, he told them.

Wilma listened to her coach, but she didn't really
hear what he said. Overconfident from her winning
streak back home in Tennessee, she thought she
would duplicate her success in Alabama. She was
wrong. Wilma Rudolph, Burt High School's unbeat-
able track star, lost every race she entered. The meet
champions were, as Coach Gray had expected, the
girls from Atlanta.

Wilma was so crushed that she withdrew into herself. She wouldn't go to any of the social events held
after the competition. While she was angry, frustrated,
and disappointed in herself, Wilma would not give up.
She realigned her energy, set aside her pride, and focused on the steps that would help her to win—just as
she had done while struggling to walk and learning to
play basketball. "I just thought to myself about how
much work was ahead of me," said Wilma.

She had previously relied on her natural ability to
win races, but Wilma admitted to herself that if she
wanted to win against world-class athletes, she would
have to concentrate on learning how to run. Just as
she had studied the finer points of basketball, so too
would she have to study the art of running. "There
was more to track than just running fast," Wilma
wrote. "I realized it was going to test me as a

person—could I come back and win again after being so totally crushed by a defeat?"

Wilma knew she would win again. Although she didn't know it then, there was also someone else who thought she would win again. Ed Temple, the well-known track coach at Tennessee State University in Nashville, had been watching Wilma closely while she ran—and lost—race after race at the Tuskegee meet.

Temple was already familiar with the spunky, gangly girl from Clarksville. Her long legs and natural athletic ability had caught his eye earlier that year as the Burt High School girls' basketball team played in the state finals. Temple was building a powerful track team—the Tigerbelles—at Tennessee State. He scouted the country for new talent, arranging a college education in exchange for an athlete's hard work, determination, and talent.

There were few opportunities for poor young black women to attend college in the 1950s. None of Wilma's siblings had attended college, and Wilma herself did not think about something as unlikely as that. But Temple knew Wilma had promise, even though he had observed her in her greatest moments of disappointing defeat. With the proper training and time to devote solely to running, he felt Wilma could become a champion.

In May 1956, Ed Temple drove from Nashville to Clarksville for a short visit with Wilma's parents. After some lengthy discussions, he persuaded the Rudolphs to let Wilma attend his summer track program for gifted

high school runners at TSU. Wilma's parents were re-
luctant to let her travel to Nashville on her own. And
Mrs. Rudolph still feared Wilma could injure herself
and hurt her right leg permanently. Coach Temple as-
sured the Rudolphs that their daughter would be all
right. She would stay in the college dorms with other
runners, and chaperones would keep a watchful eye
on her. The college would pay for everything. Wilma
needed only to pack her bags and be ready in a week.

Coach Temple himself returned to Clarksville and
drove Wilma to Nashville. Etched in Wilma's mind as
the site of her painful medical treatments, Nashville
continued to offer hope to the southern country girl
from a poor family.

The schedule at TSU was rigorous. Practice began at
6 A.M. and lasted throughout the day, with breaks between long stretches of running. Wilma and the other
athletes ran one hundred miles a week. Wilma got
along well with the other girls. More than anything—
more than winning, sometimes—Wilma wanted to be
liked by her teammates. While she took the summer
program seriously, the mentality of the high school
playdays was ingrained in her. She wanted everyone
to get along and have fun. If Wilma thought beating a
certain teammate would cause hard feelings, she'd
simply pull back at the end of the race and let the
other runner win.

Coach Temple expected his runners to be on time to
every practice and to run their best. Wilma, who was

the youngest runner in the program, was late for practice once—and only once. Temple made Wilma run thirty extra laps for being tardy. From then on, Wilma was early for every practice, just as she had been in high school.

At TSU, Wilma learned the basics of running for the first time. She learned to relax her muscles and to lean into the race as she ran around the track. Coach Temple taught his runners how to warm up before a race and the best way to breathe when they ran. Most important for Wilma, he helped her develop concentration. A perfect mix of relaxation and concentration was the formula for sprinting success.

Coach Temple also worked with Wilma on her starts, introducing her to starting blocks. Runners use starting blocks to help them push off—and start faster—at the beginning of a race. Unlike Temple's other lessons, starting blocks did not help Wilma at all. For the rest of her running career, Wilma would be a slow starter. She relied on her powerful legs to catch up to runners who had started well.

Fifteen-year-old Wilma took her newfound knowledge to various track meets around the country that summer. She found herself traveling around the South and as far as Oklahoma to compete in meets. While the TSU girls were winning races on the track, the segregated South still did not welcome them in many restaurants and gas stations because of their color. On the road, they ate brown-bag lunches from school.

When the team arrived in Philadelphia, Pennsylvania, to compete in the national Amateur Athletic Union (AAU) track meet, Wilma was immediately overwhelmed by the vast northern city. She was self-conscious of her small-town upbringing and embarrassed by her strong southern accent. "Everything in Philadelphia seemed so foreign to me," Wilma said. "The buildings seemed so big, so awesome, I was intimidated. When we went to the stadium—Franklin Field—I nearly fainted. I had never seen a stadium that big before, and I actually felt like a midget."

But Wilma didn't let the intimidation she felt upset the progress she had made. The grueling summer paid off. Wilma won all nine of the races she entered, and the TSU program won the meet's junior title. "For me, personally, I think that weekend turned the whole Tuskegee episode around," Wilma wrote. "I was confident again, and those victories helped wipe out the memory of those losses earlier."

To top off the event, Wilma and her teammates were introduced to Jackie Robinson, a famous baseball player who was in Philadelphia at the same time. Robinson was the first black in major league baseball when he joined the Brooklyn Dodgers in 1947. For years Robinson suffered insults, rough play, and even death threats as he played with his white teammates. Blacks across the nation were struggling for a fair and equal opportunity to live and work in a world that they hoped would judge people by their skills and abilities rather than the color of their skin. Jackie Robinson was an inspiration to all blacks working to end segregation.

Wilma's meeting with Robinson marked the first time she came face-to-face with a black person—aside from her family members—whom she could look up to as a hero. While the athletes posed for photographers, Robinson encouraged Wilma. "I really like your style of running," he told her. "You have a lot of potential. Don't let anything, or anybody, keep you from running."

Jackie Robinson played for the Brooklyn Dodgers as the first black player in major league baseball. A chance meeting in 1956 gave Wilma her first hero.

Wilma, second from left in the second row, *is pictured with the qualifiers for the 1956 Olympics.*

Chapter **FIVE**

"BRONZE DOESN'T SHINE"

SOON AFTER **WILMA'S** SWEEPING VICTORIES IN Philadelphia, Coach Temple asked her to accompany the Tigerbelles to the Olympic trials in Seattle, Washington. The 1956 Games were scheduled for Melbourne, Australia, in November and December.

Eager to please her coach, Wilma—a junior in high school—didn't stop to consider what it meant to compete in the Olympics. Trusting Temple's judgment without question, she packed her bags and joined the Tigerbelles as they drove cross-country with their coach. In fact, Wilma did not understand what the Olympics even were. She just assumed they were one of many important competitions that her coach wanted her to be part of. Only as Wilma began talking with her TSU teammates did she realize the Olympics were a worldwide, prestigious event, with very stiff competition.

A bit overwhelmed by the activity and travel, Wilma was grateful for the attention she received from the older runners who looked after her. One runner in particular, Mae Faggs, helped sixteen-year-old Wilma. Faggs was a stocky, powerful athlete who had already competed in the 1948 and 1952 Olympics. Nicknamed Little Mae, Faggs came from a poor black family like Wilma did and used athletics to advance her future.

Mae seemed to always be by Wilma's side, giving advice and boosting her confidence. Like Ed Temple and Jackie Robinson, Faggs recognized in Wilma the grace, talent, and determination of a world-class athlete. She took Wilma aside and told her to compete as an individual and not to worry about friendships with her teammates. Faggs sensed that Wilma, anxious about creating bad feelings among her teammates, was holding back during races and not giving her all. "Other than Coach Temple, I owe everything also to Mae," Rudolph once said. "She guided me around. I didn't know about anything when I first started, and she was like my mother. Everything I wanted to know or wanted to do I went to Mae for it."

When the Tigerbelles arrived in Seattle, Wilma was surprised by the cold weather; it was so unlike what she was used to in Tennessee. She was afraid it would affect her running. Before the qualifying heat for the 200-

meter race, Faggs gave Wilma a pep talk. "All you have to do to make this team is stick with me," she said. "You stick with me in the race, you make the team."

Wilma swallowed hard and nodded nervously. A knot was forming in her stomach, and she was nauseous and a little dizzy. She had been so nervous in the few days before the qualifying races that she could barely eat. But Faggs's pep talk steadied her.

Finally it was time for the race. The runners lined up, the starter fired a pistol, and the Olympic hopefuls raced around the track. Faggs and Wilma were neck and neck, with Wilma pulling past Faggs and then falling back until the two runners crossed the finish line at almost exactly the same time. After the race, a breathless Faggs jokingly told Wilma, "I told you to stick with me; I didn't tell you to pass me!"

Wilma made the U.S. Olympic team that year, qualifying for two events, the 200-meter race and the 400-meter relay. At sixteen she was the youngest member of the team that would compete in Melbourne, Australia, at the end of the year. She and the Tigerbelles set some impressive records in Seattle. Never before had a university placed six people from its program on an Olympic squad at the same time. Furthermore, the relay team was made up entirely of Tigerbelles—another Olympic first.

Clarksville was buzzing with the news when Wilma returned from Seattle. Wilma was about to travel farther from home than most citizens from Clarksville

Wilma, left, *crossed the finish line just behind Mae Faggs,* right, *in the Seattle, Washington, trials for the U.S. Women's Olympic track team, 1956.*

had ever dreamed of going. Uncertain and inexperienced, she relied on Coach Temple and Mae Faggs to get her ready for overseas travel. Temple obtained her passport, and Faggs held on to it. Wilma was afraid she might lose it. Without a passport, she would have difficulty leaving the country and getting back home.

Knowing that the Rudolphs didn't have the money to buy necessary items for a long trip overseas, some Clarksville merchants gave Wilma clothes and luggage to take to Melbourne. "I have never forgotten those people to this day," Wilma wrote in her autobiography. "I love them dearly for the help they gave me when I most needed it." Before Wilma left for the airport, the citizens of Clarksville gave her a small send-off ceremony to wish her good luck in Melbourne.

When Wilma boarded the airplane in Nashville, headed for two weeks of training in Los Angeles, she was embarking on her first airplane ride. When the flight attendant served the meal, Wilma declined because she had no money to pay for it. Faggs, knowing Wilma didn't understand the food was free, quietly explained to her that refreshments on the trip were included with her ticket. Only then did Wilma accept a meal tray. But her stomach was so upset, like it had been at the Olympic trials, that she couldn't eat. The other Tigerbelles picked at her tray until the food was gone.

The two weeks in Los Angeles passed quickly. Although Coach Temple did not accompany the Olympic team to Los Angeles and would not be in Melbourne, he had prepared written training instructions for his Tigerbelles. Olympic Coach Nell Jackson, the U.S. Olympic team's first black female coach, followed Temple's instructions during the training.

When the runners weren't training, Wilma eagerly listened to Faggs's stories about the Olympics. The veteran runner explained the history of the Games and told Wilma that when they arrived in Melbourne, they would make friends with athletes from around the world. Faggs also said that more than the medals she had won, she valued the friendships she had made along with the experience of traveling. Wilma would soon find out, Mae promised her.

There were also other aspects of the trip Wilma would discover. Australia was on the other side of the world. Although winter had arrived in the United States, November and December were summer months in the world's Southern Hemisphere.

At last it was time to board the plane for the two-day journey to Melbourne. Wilma was grateful that basketball player Bill Russell looked out for her. "He used to watch over me like I was his daughter," she remembered. "He knew I was the youngest person on the U.S. team and he wanted to make sure that nothing happened to me. He was beautiful."

The trip exposed Wilma to cultures she had never known or thought about. "I began to realize that the world was bigger than Clarksville," Wilma remembered. "I said to myself, 'You're lucky, you're luckier than all of the kids back home, because you're getting to see all of these things and they're not.'"

The team had extended layovers in Hawaii and then the Fiji Islands. Wilma was fascinated by the tropical cultures. When the athletes walked off the plane in Hawaii, they were greeted by native islanders who presented them with garlands of flowers. In Fiji, Wilma was amazed to see a country of black citizens.

In Hawaii, which was then a territory of the United States and not yet a state, Wilma was reminded that many people still considered blacks to be second-class citizens. She and the other members of the women's Olympic track team were window shopping in Honolulu when a white woman crossed the street to avoid walking near them, then told them they shouldn't be allowed in public. "That made me sad for the rest of the day," Wilma said. "We all felt sad because, here we were, members of the United States Olympic Team, and that didn't really matter at all because we were still black, no matter what we did."

When the team boarded the plane for the last part of the trip, Wilma thought about how far she had come. Five years earlier she could barely walk, much less run. Now she was flying halfway across the world to compete in the most prestigious athletic competition. Her stomach flip-flopped as she experienced a full range of feelings—happiness, nervousness, and fear.

When the athletes arrived in Melbourne, the weather was cold and rainy. Wilma made the best of the dreary climate and enjoyed meeting athletes from other countries. She knew she was fortunate to have an opportunity to compete in the Olympics, and she wanted to experience it to the fullest. Fans lingered outside of the Olympic Village, hoping to collect autographs from the American athletes. Sometimes Wilma and her teammates stood for two hours signing autographs. She met many people of color—Mexicans, Asians, and Africans. She also heard many accents and became less self-conscious of her own. During training the Australian starter visited with the athletes so they could familiarize themselves with his accent and understand him when he started each race.

WOMEN IN THE OLYMPICS

While women participate in nearly all Olympic events, the presence of female athletes in the most prestigious global sports competition has been a hard-won victory. In ancient Greece, where the Olympic Games originated, sports were an important part of daily life for all children—although girls and boys participated in separate competitions. Girls and women were barred altogether from the Olympic Games, however. Females could not even watch the Games. The first Olympic competitions were held in Greece in 776 B.C. Men competed until the ancient Games ceased around A.D. 400. Almost fifteen hundred years later, the first modern Olympic Games were held in Athens in 1896. Again, women were banned from participating.

In the year 1896, a woman's place was definitely not in the sports arena. Women had few rights, but feminists around the world were standing up to the societies that restricted them. Women had begun to work for the right to vote and to hold property. Some women wanted access to more educational opportunities and to the workplace. Others demanded the right to hold political office and to be socially and financially independent. Over the next several decades, women in England, the United States, Japan, Russia, and Brazil secured these rights.

In the early 1900s, women were still considered the "fairer sex." Doctors warned women against overexerting their bodies and brains by working outside the home, participating in politics, or playing sports. Some people believed sports could make women infertile. (This same argument was not applied to men.) Although women did participate in recreational sports such as croquet, golf, and ice skating, they were considered unladylike if they beat a male opponent. Women played their sports in long skirts, which severely restricted their movements.

Women were allowed to compete in the 1900 Olympic Games in Paris, France, but were limited to the less strenuous events of lawn tennis, yachting, and golf. Track-and-field events remained a men's sport until 1928, when three women's events were added. The introduction of women's track and field brought harsh criticism. Even Pope Pius XI weighed in against the decision.

Wilma and the 1960 women's 100-meter dash Olympic medalists

Unfortunately, several female competitors collapsed after running the 800-meter race in the 1928 Games, and track events longer than 200 meters were then closed to women. It wasn't until 1960—the year Wilma Rudolph won three gold medals in Rome—that women were again permitted to run longer races. It would be another twenty-four years (1984) before the women's marathon was introduced. In 1932, the multitalented American, Mildred "Babe" Didrikson won five events at the Olympic trials. Each victory should have entitled her to advance to the Olympics in that event. Female athletes, however, were permitted to participate in only three events at the Olympics. While women were making headway into the male-dominated sports arena, they still faced restrictions imposed by Olympic officials who lacked confidence in the abilities and stamina of women.

As the modern Olympic Games developed, and as the world slowly changed its view of women's roles, more and more women's events were added. In recent years, the International Olympic Committee has continued to add women's events—judo in 1992, soccer in 1996, and ice hockey in 1998.

The week before the competition began, Wilma trained, visited with the other athletes in the Olympic Village, and enjoyed the food. She particularly enjoyed her conversations with Australian runner Betty Cuthbert. The eighteen-year-old Cuthbert and Wilma were close in age and, despite the differences between them, the two athletes clicked. Cuthbert was favored to win several women's track events, but that didn't intimidate Wilma or stop her from picking up pointers from her talented competitor. From Cuthbert she learned about a new women's running shoe made in Australia of soft kangaroo leather. It would help her race, Cuthbert told Wilma, because it was lighter than traditional running shoes. Wilma wanted a pair badly but didn't have the twenty dollars to buy them.

When it came time for the qualifying race for the 200-meter dash, Wilma lined up with the other athletes. The race started, and Wilma ran her best— finishing third. She moved to the semifinals, where she finished third again. Although she had run well, only the top two could advance to the finals. Wilma would not get her chance to compete for Olympic gold in the 200-meter race. Devastated, she convinced herself she was a failure. Suddenly, she missed Coach Temple more than ever. She had come to rely on him heavily to give her pointers and strengthen her concentration.

Despite her disappointment, Wilma forced herself to watch the remaining track events. From the sidelines,

Wilma's experience in Melbourne, Australia, was her first with fans. Sometimes she and her teammates stood for hours signing autographs. Throughout her entire career, Wilma never turned down an autograph.

she watched Betty Cuthbert win three gold medals. Cuthbert's wins renewed Wilma's determination. She vowed to return to the Olympics in 1960 and win a gold medal. "You've got four years to get there yourself," she told herself.

Then came Wilma's other event, the 400-meter relay. The Tigerbelles who made up the team had practiced poorly, and they were concerned about their sloppy baton passing. On the day of the race, however, Mae Faggs gave them all a pep talk that helped them concentrate. As expected, Australia took first in 44.5 seconds, smashing the world record by four-tenths of a second. Great Britain came in second in 44.7, and the United States was third at 44.9.

Wilma had mixed feelings about her bronze medal as she stood on the winner's box with her relay teammates. She was pleased that she had placed, but she

Wilma was inspired watching Betty Cuthbert, right, *and she vowed to return to the 1960 Olympics and win a gold medal. Here Betty is pictured with Bobby Morrow, the men's 100-meter gold medalist in the 1956 Olympic Games.*

was keenly aware that she wasn't bringing home the gold. "What will the people of Clarksville think?" Wilma wondered.

Wilma had nothing to worry about. She was welcomed home as a hero. The Burt High principal closed school for the day and held a special assembly with Wilma as the guest of honor. Speaking in front of the entire school made her more nervous than flying all the way to Australia and running in the Olympics. All her classmates wanted to see and touch her medal. She passed it around during the assembly, proud to share a little piece of the world with her friends in Clarksville. When the last person had admired the medal and handed it back to Wilma, she noticed it was smudged with fingerprints. She rubbed it against her clothes to bring back the shine.

"I started shining it up," she said. "And I discovered that bronze doesn't shine. So I decided, 'I'm going to try this one more time. I'm going for the gold.'"

Wilma's life changed after she became an Olympic medalist. Wilma is pictured with the 1956 400-meter relay bronze medalists. From left to right: *Margaret Matthews, Wilma, Mae Faggs, and Isabelle Daniels.*

Chapter SIX

CHANGES

SETTLING BACK INTO HIGH SCHOOL AND HER DAILY routine, Wilma soon learned that her life had changed because she had become an Olympic medalist. Her friends acted differently around her. Suddenly they didn't know how to treat Clarksville's most famous citizen. Inside, Wilma felt like the same Wilma she had always been. She was Skeeter, who loved basketball, running, and hanging out with her friends. Some kids made mean remarks to and about her. "They either put you on a pedestal, or else they put you down," Wilma wrote in her autobiography. "There was no in-between."

After Wilma had returned from Melbourne, Coach Gray proudly allowed her to start Burt High's basketball season, even though she had missed weeks of practices. She led the team to the state title that year, averaging 35 points a game.

"I always felt people expected me to do better than that because I had been on the Olympic team," Wilma said. "I put a lot of pressure on myself, I guess, and I spent a lot of time looking over my shoulder, wondering if people were saying bad things about me, and feeling that a lot of them would be happy if I failed."

At the end of the basketball season, during the game for the state title, Wilma made a mistake just seconds before the game ended. She passed the ball away and allowed the opposing team a chance to score. Even though the clock sounded before the other team scored, preserving Burt High's victory, Coach Gray was furious. He yelled at Wilma and called her stupid in front of her teammates and the bleachers full of fans. Humiliated and angry, Wilma stormed off the court.

Wilma was hurt and confused by Coach Gray's behavior, and although Coach Gray apologized and they soon made up, his tongue-lashing stung Wilma for the rest of her life. When she returned from Melbourne, she never expected that her coach would be among her biggest critics.

Conditions didn't improve during the track season, either. Some team members and opponents refused to run against the girl who had won an Olympic bronze medal. Without even trying, they decided that she couldn't be beat. With less competition, Wilma continued her winning streak.

*Clinton Gray coached
Wilma in both
basketball and track
throughout high
school.*

But the winning didn't make Wilma feel as good as
it had the previous year. During her junior year of
high school, Wilma felt like an outcast. If it hadn't
been for family, her boyfriend, Robert Eldridge, and
her best friend, Nancy Bowen, she would have felt
completely alone.

The end of her junior year was a special time for
Wilma, because it held the long-anticipated prom. For

years she and Robert had fantasized about attending the junior-senior prom together, and finally, the magical evening arrived. Wilma's parents couldn't afford to buy her a prom dress, so she borrowed a dark blue gown and adorned it with a white orchid Robert gave her. They drove off in a new two-tone blue Ford that Robert borrowed from his father. "We showed up at the high school gym in fine style," Wilma remembered.

After the dance, Wilma, Robert, and their friends, including Nancy Bowen, drove to a Kentucky nightclub where bartenders would serve alcohol to teenagers. When the place grew rowdy, the Clarksville kids left and dared each other to race home. Robert and Wilma sped away in Mr. Eldridge's new Ford, making it back well before the others. Nancy and the remaining kids piled into two other cars. The two drivers decided to drag, racing side-by-side on a two-lane highway. Speeding at ninety miles an hour, the driver of the car Nancy was in lost control and hit a concrete pillar. Nancy and the driver were killed instantly. Three other riders were seriously injured.

A distraught Coach Gray delivered the news to Wilma early the next morning. He had thought she and Nancy were riding together and was sure Wilma was dead too. He repeated over and over again, "Thank God you're alive."

The news left Wilma limp and empty. "Nancy's was my first experience with tragedy," she said. "I couldn't handle it. I was an emotional wreck for weeks."

A grieving Wilma eagerly awaited the end of school, when she could return to TSU for summer track training. She believed a change of scenery would help her cope with the loss of her friend. At first, being in Nashville and away from the memories of Nancy made little difference. She couldn't concentrate. Coach Temple, who had known Nancy from the basketball games he officiated, sympathized with Wilma. But that didn't stop him from pushing her hard those months.

"He knew what my problem was," Wilma remembered. "But he also knew that only time could heal a wound such as that. Slowly, I started coming out of it." The summer was good for Wilma and helped take her mind off Nancy's death.

Soon after Wilma returned to high school for her senior year, she visited Dr. Coleman for her annual physical. After the exam, Dr. Coleman, who had encouraged her when she was a young girl struggling to overcome polio, sat Wilma down and gave her some shocking news. Seventeen-year-old Wilma was pregnant.

Wilma stared at the doctor, dumbfounded. She and Robert were in love and had experimented with sex only a few times, but they hadn't understood they could use birth control methods to avoid pregnancy. Wilma and her classmates did not have sex education classes, and the Rudolphs—strict Baptists—did not discuss such subjects with their children. "I couldn't ask [my parents] about such things as sex, because sex was a taboo subject in the religion," Wilma said. "A lot of things I wanted to know more about back then, and I should have been able to go to my mother for the answers. But I never did."

Abortions were illegal in the 1950s, and Wilma wouldn't have considered having one if they had been legal. Her only option was to have the baby and either keep it or give it up for adoption. "In those days . . . nobody was sent away to live with an aunt for a while like the white girls did," Wilma wrote in her autobiography. "The black girls stayed in school pregnant, like nothing was wrong at all."

Ashamed of herself and her predicament, Wilma hid her pregnancy for almost two months, continuing her life as if nothing had changed. How could she tell her parents and her coaches about what she'd done? They all expected great things of her in the 1960 Olympic Games. For two long, sad months, Wilma believed her athletic career was over. She knew Coach Temple did not allow mothers into his track program at TSU, and without him Wilma could not go to college or the Olympics. Part of Wilma believed that if she ignored the pregnancy, it might go away. Finally, Coach Gray noticed that Wilma's stomach was growing. He persuaded Wilma to tell her parents.

Mr. and Mrs. Rudolph surprised her with their reaction. They told her that everyone makes mistakes and that she should not be ashamed of her pregnancy. Even so, Mr. Rudolph forbade Wilma from seeing

Robert again; he blamed Robert for the pregnancy. Robert had wanted Wilma to marry him, but she turned him down. Wilma felt she would never realize her dream of going to college and making something of herself if she became a wife at such a young age. Her father also adamantly rejected the idea of the marriage, and Wilma didn't want to do anything else to hurt her family. After Wilma rejected Robert's proposal, he distanced himself from her and even began dating another girl. "That really destroyed me, because I felt that now he was deserting me just as my whole world was about to collapse."

But perhaps the biggest surprise of all came from Coach Temple. He heard a rumor about Wilma from the TSU Tigerbelles and drove to Clarksville to find out the truth for himself. One look at Wilma confirmed that she was, indeed, expecting a baby. "I went and hid," Wilma remembered of Temple's visit.

"I couldn't face him." But Wilma's parents made her come back and talk with Temple. And she was glad she did. Temple made an exception to his rule about mothers in his track program. He told Wilma he still wanted her at TSU after the baby was born. "The scholarship was waiting for me at Tennessee State in September, and all I had to do was give birth and then start running on my own to get back in shape," Wilma remembered.

After all the obstacles she had faced, Wilma knew that with the love and support of her family and her

Coach Temple expected his runners to work hard on the track as well as in the classroom, requiring a B average from all of them. It paid off. Of the forty Olympians Ed Temple coached, thirty-nine earned one or more college degrees.

coach, she could face what lay ahead. Suddenly Wilma's world wasn't collapsing after all. "The people I loved were sticking by me, and that alone took a lot of pressure, and pain, and guilt, off my shoulders," she said.

Wilma finished high school along with several other girls who were also pregnant. There was no stigma attached to her pregnancy, she said later. But Wilma did have to quit the basketball team immediately. She also had to sit out her senior-year track season. She graduated in June, seven months pregnant. In July she gave birth to a daughter, Yolanda.

Wilma knew she couldn't balance the demands of school, running, and parenting. Caring for a newborn would also be too difficult for Wilma's aging parents. Wilma, her sister Yvonne, and their mother agreed that Yvonne could care for Yolanda while Wilma was at school. Yvonne was married and living in St. Louis, Missouri, and she had the time and energy to care for the baby.

After a year and a half marked by tragedy and life-altering changes, Wilma set off for college—where she would study elementary education to become a teacher. Her dream of becoming an official Tigerbelle had come true.

Wilma had to work hard in college. To maintain the B average that Coach Temple required of all Tigerbelles, Wilma could no longer cut class to practice running. She also had to work part-time in the campus post office to earn her room and board. Her days were overflowing with school, work, training, and meets. She rarely saw Yolanda. Although Wilma was a mother, Coach Temple refused to treat her differently from her teammates.

The Tigerbelles had two years to prepare for the 1960 Summer Olympics to be held in Rome, Italy, and Coach Temple didn't want his runners distracted. The Olympic clock was ticking.

Wilma crosses the finish line in the 400-meter relay to win her third gold medal in the 1960 Summer Olympics.

Chapter SEVEN

GOING FOR THE GOLD

IN 1959 WILMA RAN WELL AND STUDIED HARD. For the most part, she was able to keep her mind on her college experiences. By Christmastime, when Coach Temple gave the athletes a few days off, Wilma was eager to see her baby daughter. But when she arrived home, her sister Yvonne had come alone, leaving Yolanda in St. Louis. Yvonne shocked Wilma by suggesting that Wilma allow her to adopt the baby.

"I absolutely panicked," Wilma said. "I never thought that my sister would want to keep my baby. I spent the rest of the day in a frenzy, thinking of ways of getting my baby back." Without her father's permission, she enlisted Robert's help. The two drove to St. Louis and brought Yolanda back to Clarksville. Even though

Mr. Rudolph was furious that Wilma had traveled all the way to St. Louis alone with Robert, he and Mrs. Rudolph insisted on keeping the baby with them. Robert's mother also stepped in to help care for Yolanda at times.

When Wilma arrived back at college, she concentrated on her studies. Her track training took so much time that she sometimes struggled to make the adjustment from high school classes to college classes. She sometimes wondered if she should quit school and track to be a full-time mother. When those moments became too powerful, Wilma would remind herself that Yolanda was in good hands. Wilma also knew if she quit, she would regret missing the chance to see how far her running abilities could take her.

During her sophomore year—the year of the Olympic trials—Wilma suddenly lost her speed. She lost race after race. No one, not even Wilma, understood what was happening. She felt fine, and even Coach Temple agreed that there was nothing flawed in her running style. When a doctor determined that a tonsil infection had been draining Wilma's strength, she and Coach Temple were relieved. Wilma underwent surgery to have her tonsils removed. Once she was back on the track, she ran faster than ever.

Wilma had never been in better shape than she was in August 1960, when she arrived in Texas to compete in the Olympic trials. When she ran in the 200-meter qualifier, she even set a world record of 22.9 seconds.

Wilma qualified for all three of her events at the 1960 Olympic trials.

That year, the twenty-year-old qualified for all three of her events, the 100-meter and 200-meter dashes and the 400-meter relay. Again there were four Tigerbelles on the women's relay team.

By the time Wilma qualified for her second Olympic Games, she had learned about a black hero she could look up to in the world of track and field. Jesse Owens had been born into a poor sharecropping family in Alabama and had gone on to win four gold medals in the 1936 Olympic Games, held in Berlin, Germany. Four years before Wilma was born, Owens faced prejudice in Berlin. German chancellor Adolf Hitler believed that his race, the Aryans, were superior to all other groups of people, especially Jews and blacks. When Owens won his four medals, he embarrassed Hitler in front of the world. In Seattle Wilma qualified for three of the same events that Owens had run in 1936. Wilma decided that her performance at the 1960 Olympics would be a tribute to Owens.

Wilma and the Tigerbelles were ecstatic when they learned that Temple would coach the U.S. Olympic track-and-field team. Having a coach they knew and loved would give the Tigerbelles an advantage in Rome. "I knew somebody up there was taking care of me this time around," Wilma said, remembering the long weeks in Australia without her mentor.

During the pre-Olympic training in Emporia, Kansas, Wilma was grateful to have Coach Temple by her side. He knew his runners inside and out. Knowing that Wilma might get burned out if she practiced three times a day like the other runners, he cut her practices down to once a day.

Coach Temple didn't want his athletes worrying about their competitors because he feared such musings would disturb their concentration. But when the Tigerbelles were out of their coach's earshot, they whispered together about Jutta Heine, a German runner whose legs were as long as Wilma's and who was winning every race she entered in Europe. Wilma was nervous, but she psyched herself up whenever doubts nagged at her. "She should be worrying about me," Wilma told herself whenever she thought of Heine.

Arriving in Rome two weeks before the Games began, Wilma was comforted by the familiar routine. She roomed with her TSU teammate, Lucinda Williams, became reacquainted with friends she hadn't seen in four years, and signed autographs for eager Italian fans. Best of all, the weather was familiar. "The hot weather actually helped put me in a good frame of mind," Wilma remembered.

For the first time in the history of the Summer Games, the events would be televised worldwide. Wilma knew her friends and family back home in Clarksville would be watching her run and cheering her on to victory. That thought energized her.

Things seemed to be going her way until a few days before her first event, when Wilma stepped into a small hole on an unofficial practice field and twisted her ankle. Immediately her foot swelled. Tears welled up in Wilma's eyes as she imagined the 1960 Olympics continuing without her. The doctor ordered her to stay off her feet. Only if she rested her sore ankle could she even hope to run.

When it was time to run the 100-meter dash, Wilma's ankle was stronger. In the minutes before the race, she joined the other runners at the Olympic stadium and lay down on a bench to rest. The 100-meter race was a straight shot down the track without the curves of the 200-meter race. Of the three events in which Wilma was entered, the 100-meter would be easiest on her strained ankle.

As the announcer called her name, Wilma emerged from the tunnel into the stadium, and the Italian crowd went wild, chanting her name over and over again. "Vilma! Vilma!" In the two weeks she had been in

Rome, the graceful, cheerful Wilma had impressed the fans with her speed and her quiet, unassuming dignity.

Wilma was touched by the reception, but she reminded herself to stay focused. "You start smiling and waving and listening to the cheering and chanting," she told herself, "you're going to forget all about the real reason you're here. To win." With her long, powerful strides, Wilma easily won her first race by three yards, leaving Jutta Heine far behind, and finishing in 11 seconds flat. Wilma's time would have been a world record if it had not been wind-aided.

Barbara Jones, one of the Tigerbelles, remembered years later how graceful Wilma's running had been. "She was so beautiful when she ran," Jones said. "And once she started working with her arms and the leaning [into the race], then the confidence came automatically and you couldn't beat her. You couldn't come close to her."

Three days later, Wilma reported for her second race—the 200-meter dash. This time, she was so relaxed that she fell asleep on a bench while she waited for her event to start. Her competitors, themselves jumbles of nervous energy, were shocked by this seemingly carefree American. In spite of the rain, Wilma won easily, but she was disappointed with, even embarrassed by, her time—24 seconds flat. "It was like walking," she scolded herself. During practices and trial heats, she had averaged 22.9 seconds.

But the world didn't care about times or records.

People from all over the globe were taken with the young woman from a small American town who was so kind and friendly and whose sparkling smile made everyone feel at ease. When Wilma arrived back at her room at the end of the day, it was filled with flowers. Betty Cuthbert, who missed the Games because of an injury, sent the first of many well-wishing telegrams Wilma would receive. The media had reported to the world that just ten years earlier Wilma could barely walk, much less run. Her victories, after years of hardship and adversity, made people love her all the more.

After the second race, Wilma believed that she had a good shot at a third gold medal. "That's two gold medals down and one to go," she told herself. She was determined to help her Tigerbelle teammates win a gold medal and to become the first American woman to win three gold medals in a single Olympics.

Her ankle was still sore though, and the curve in the last event, the 400-meter relay, would test her strength. Wilma's bursts of speed would be more important than ever. She would be running the last 100-meter leg of the race—the anchor leg—because she was the team's fastest runner, and the fate of the race depended on her performance. The Tigerbelles would face stiff competition from the Soviet and German runners. The Americans had one advantage, though. They had been running together as a team for months, practicing the crucial passing of the baton from runner to runner. The runners knew one another and what each runner could accomplish. Their world-record time of 44.4 seconds in the semifinals gave the team extra confidence heading into the final race.

The women's relay took place on September 7, 1960, the last day of the Summer Olympics. The crowd of eighty thousand spectators was vibrating with anxious energy. The race began smoothly. After the first three legs of the race, the Americans were in the lead. Then it was Wilma's turn. She stretched her arm out behind her to receive the baton from teammate Lucinda Williams. As she began running, Wilma nearly dropped the baton, losing precious time as she stopped to grasp it. If she had dropped it, the American team would have been disqualified.

The fumbling cost the team dearly. When Wilma started her leg of the race, the Americans were in fourth place; the other runners were three or four yards ahead. But Wilma was used to coming from behind, and she knew how to run against the odds. With the same steady determination that had helped her overcome childhood illnesses, Wilma threw herself into the race, passing Jutta Heine of Germany and Halina Richter of Poland to win her third gold medal. It was a photo finish. The Tigerbelles finished the race in 44.5 seconds, just a fraction of a second behind their day-old world record. "When I broke the tape, I had my three gold medals, and the feeling of accomplishment welled up inside of me," Wilma remembered.

Years later Coach Temple remembered how proud

Wilma was that she had helped the other Tigerbelles win their gold medals. "I think she took more joy in that relay than she did in her individual events," he said.

Photographs of Wilma's 1960 performance show her long legs, how she leaned her entire body into the race, and how she pumped her arms. Her facial expressions are a mixture of pain and determination. One reporter described it this way: "There is struggle on her face. There is the hint of a smile, certainly, but it's the wince, the urgent reaching, the pain of unmet desire that catches the eye."

After Wilma stepped down from the victory stand, newspaper reporters mobbed her, jostling one another to get closer to the fastest woman in the world. Everyone wanted to hear from Wilma. The *New York Times* called her the World Speed Queen, and other American papers dubbed her the Tennessee Tornado. Coach Temple began calling her the Jesse Owens of women's track and field. The French press nicknamed her *La Gazelle Noire* (the black gazelle). Wilma was proud to be compared to the graceful animal. "I didn't find it offensive at all," Wilma said of the nickname, "because I knew they weren't just speaking of color. They were speaking of something beautiful in color and motion."

As Wilma was led away from the mob of reporters, her third gold medal hanging around her neck, an Olympic official told her, "Wilma, life will never be the same for you again." Millions of fans across the world had rooted for Wilma as she ran and won her three

Wilma with the U.S. team after they won the gold medal for the women's 400-meter relay race. From left to right: *Wilma, Barbara P. Jones, Lucinda Williams, and Martha Hudson.*

events. Her face would become as familiar to them as the faces of movie stars and musicians.

Almost immediately after winning her third gold medal, Wilma noticed a change in the other American athletes, even among her own Tigerbelle teammates. They were upset that Wilma was receiving all the media attention, especially since the relay had been a team event. The events of 1956, when her classmates treated her differently upon her return from the Melbourne Olympics, seemed to be repeating themselves.

Instead of returning home immediately, Coach Temple took the Tigerbelles on a monthlong tour of Europe, where they competed in scores of races for adoring fans. Everywhere they went, they were greeted by hundreds of people who wanted to see Wilma.

"[Fans] would rock the bus when we pulled in," Temple remembered. "If [Wilma] put her track shoes down, someone would pick them up and be gone with them. She couldn't let loose of anything. But she never turned down a single autograph."

Wilma's growing celebrity only increased tension among the Tigerbelles. One evening before a banquet in England, the Tigerbelles hid the hair curlers from Wilma, and she had to go out with disheveled hair. Another time they purposely ran slowly in a relay so Wilma would lose. Their plan backfired when Wilma came from forty meters behind to win the race.

The jealousy and petty arguing wore Wilma down. She was also completely exhausted by the constant activity and unyielding attention from the media. She confided to a reporter from the *New York Times,* "I'm beat. I've lost twelve pounds since I got to Rome and I still have a cold I caught in Germany."

Most of all, she was homesick for her family, especially two-year-old Yolanda. The Rudolphs had constant word of Wilma because they could read about her in the newspaper, hear her voice on radio, and see her on television. But Wilma was isolated from them. "I had three gold medals, and now I wanted to share them with the people I loved most," she said.

It was time to go home.

Wilma's three gold medals from the 1960 Olympics made her an international star.

Chapter EIGHT

"I KNEW WHAT TIME IT WAS"

EXHAUSTED AFTER THE OLYMPICS AND AN ADDITIONAL
month of touring, all Wilma wanted was to return
home to Clarksville for a well-earned rest and reunion
with her family. When she arrived in Nashville,
though, Temple told her she'd have to stay put for a
few days while her hometown organized a homecoming celebration for her. Wilma agreed to stay with the
Temples in the meantime, but that night she sneaked
out of their house and persuaded a friend to give her
a ride to Clarksville so she could see her family. Then
Wilma sneaked back into the Temples' home before
they knew she was gone.

When Wilma officially arrived in Clarksville, she understood why the planning of her homecoming had

Wilma, second from left, *with her mother, father, and younger sister Charlene when she returned home after winning three gold medals.*

taken so long. As she rode in a parade down Clarksville's main street, throngs of people—white and black—lined both sides of the streets. City leaders had been planning Clarksville's first integrated event—and that took some doing. More than three thousand people turned out to welcome Wilma home.

"Our pride stems not alone from your victories," Clarksville mayor William Barksdale told Wilma. "Rather, we are proud that you retained your simple modesty, graciousness, and dignity in victory. These are the marks of your greatness."

The celebration continued into the evening when more than one thousand of the town's citizens attended a banquet held in Wilma's honor. Again blacks and whites were in attendance, dining side by side and enjoying the evening's program. When Wilma got up to speak, she faced her hometown audience and thanked them for their faith in her. "Amid my happiness, I am aware of the responsibilities that go along with being a champion," she said. "In every effort, I have been motivated by one thing—to do justice to those who believe in me and to use my physical talents to the glory of God and the honor of womanhood."

Of all the toasts and speeches made that night, Wilma remembered one in particular. An elderly retired judge raised his glass and said:

> Ladies and gentlemen, you play a piano. You can play very nice music on a piano by playing only the black keys on it, and you can play very nice music on the same piano by playing only the white keys on it. But ladies and gentlemen, the absolute best music comes out of that piano when you play both the black keys and the white keys together.

That night Wilma knew she had won another victory—perhaps more important than what she had accomplished in Rome. Her homecoming ushered in a new era in Clarksville, and she was proud to have been a part of the change.

Wilma realized quickly how much her life had changed. She was almost never left alone—a steady stream of well-wishers, reporters, and photographers invaded the Rudolph household. She had already met several important people, including Pope John XXIII, the head of the Roman Catholic Church. Before long TSU arranged for the Tigerbelles to tour the United States, making appearances and running in special meets. Wilma met famous people and important political and diplomatic figures. In Chicago, Mayor Richard J. Daley presented Wilma with the keys to the city. In Washington, D.C., Wilma and her mother had an informal and friendly meeting with President John F. Kennedy in the White House. "It's really an honor to meet you and tell you what a magnificent runner you are," the president told Wilma.

In Louisville, Kentucky, Wilma rode in a parade with Cassius Clay (who would change his name to Muhammad Ali in 1964). Clay had also competed in the 1960 Olympic Games, winning a gold medal in the light heavyweight boxing division. "I took great pride in introducing her to my family and friends," Ali remembered years later. "I was thankful to God that I had the opportunity to meet her."

"It was one big social whirl, and I was getting spoiled rotten," Wilma said. "I didn't even do my own hair; everywhere I went, somebody did it for me, and it never cost me a cent."

Officials of major track meets invited Wilma to run in events planned especially for her. Wilma's presence at the New York Athletic Club, the Millrose Games, the Penn Relays, and the Drake Relays was important

President Kennedy chatted with Wilma in his White House office on April 14, 1961.

because women had never participated in them before. "I was the first, and the doors have been open ever since to women," Wilma said. "I'm proud of that to this day."

And the awards came rolling in. In 1961 Wilma was named the Woman Athlete of the Year. Italy gave her its Christopher Columbus award, recognizing her as the best international athlete of the year. She was the first American to receive the award. In the United States, Wilma won the James E. Sullivan Award, the most prestigious honor given to amateur athletes. She was the first black woman to receive the award.

Despite her celebrity status, Wilma still worried about money. Gold medalists in the 1960s were not guaranteed product endorsements and the six- to eight-figure income that star athletes have come to command. Nor could Wilma plan on a future in athletics. Professional

Twenty-one-year-old Wilma is shown here with William Ward, with whom she had a brief marriage in 1961.

opportunities in sports were rare for women at that time. While the TSU alumni society paid for Wilma's tour around the country, she returned to her old job at the post office when she arrived back on campus to resume her classes.

Soon the fastest woman in the world began to consider her future. So much had happened in the previous year. She had met the president of the United States and scores of other celebrities. She had traveled throughout the United States and Europe. She had continued to race, breaking world records and setting new ones. She had also had a brief marriage to fellow TSU student and athlete William Ward. "Where do I go from here?" she asked herself.

Already, when she lost a race, newspapers ran huge headlines suggesting that something was wrong with her. Her fans expected her to win all the time. Wilma thought that if she didn't win in the 1964 Olympics, the world would remember her defeat rather than her victories. She didn't want that to happen. Coach Temple agreed. And so it was decided. Wilma Rudolph, the star of the 1960 Olympics, would retire from competitive running in 1962, after a race against Soviet runners at Stanford University. But first she had to win.

She won the 100-meter race with ease. The 400-meter relay would be more difficult, however. Again, Wilma ran the anchor. Wilma admitted that the Soviets were better relay runners. Sure enough, when it was Wilma's turn to run with the baton, the Soviet anchor runner was forty yards ahead of her. But that didn't stop Wilma.

"I give chase, I start picking up speed, and I start closing on her," she said. "She's looking at me out of the corner of her eye. . . . Well, I caught her, passed her, and won the race. That was it. The crowd in the stadium was on its feet, giving me a standing ovation, and I knew what time it was. Time to retire, with a sweet taste."

After the race, Wilma was mobbed by fans. She patiently signed autographs until the crowd dispersed and only one fan remained. A little boy holding a small piece of paper and a pencil shyly approached Wilma and asked for her autograph. "Son, I'll do better than that," she said. She produced a ballpoint pen from her bag and signed her track shoes. Then she gave the shoes to the surprised boy.

"I didn't hang up my spikes, I gave them away," Wilma said.

Wilma and approximately three hundred African-Americans sought unsuccessfully to be served at a drive-in restaurant in her hometown in 1963.

Chapter **NINE**

STRUGGLES

AFTER RETIRING FROM COMPETITIVE TRACK, WILMA returned to college to finish her degree. But, as she had already learned, life would never be the same—whether she was running or not. She made several trips abroad as a goodwill ambassador on behalf of the U.S. government and other organizations. She traveled to Africa and Japan.

During this busy time in her life, Wilma lost a good friend and mentor. Coach Gray was killed in a car accident in Clarksville in 1962. The news shocked and saddened Wilma. Although her first coach had at times been a harsh critic, she had loved him nonetheless.

Although she wanted to attend Coach Gray's funeral, a friend and former teacher talked her out of

Wilma graduated from Tennessee State University on May 27, 1963.

postponing her international tour. "Coach Gray would have wanted you to go," she told Wilma. "After all, he started you on this life."

In May 1963, twenty-three-year-old Wilma graduated from college with a degree in education. She already had a job lined up in Clarksville, teaching second grade at Cobb Elementary and coaching girls' track at Burt High. While Wilma could have lived anywhere and taken nearly any job, she was genuinely looking forward to returning to the only home she had ever known. Returning to Clarksville also meant she could work to end segregation in her hometown.

Finally, in the summer of 1963, after a very long and tumultuous courtship, Wilma and Robert were married. In the next two years, Wilma gave birth to two children, Djuana, a girl, in May 1964 and Robert Jr. in August 1965. Like other recent college graduates, newlyweds, and new mothers, Wilma experienced many stresses. She worked hard to support her children and Robert, who was still in college. Although Wilma loved teaching and coaching, the job also frustrated her. Her colleagues, many of them the same teachers who had taught there while she was growing up, resisted her innovations. "My idea of teaching was to bring new ideas into the classroom; after all, that's what I went to college for, to learn new ideas and methods. But they wanted to stay the same, no change, and they resisted everything I tried to do."

By 1965 Wilma knew she needed a change. During the next several years, she moved from job to job, hoping to find one that was just right. Wilma wanted to create in her career the feelings of certainty and confidence that she had felt in running. Unfortunately, that took a long time to happen. Wilma's many jobs took her young family around the country. In Indiana she worked as a director of a community center. In Maine she ran a girls' physical education program.

In 1967 Vice President Hubert Humphrey invited Wilma to work for Operation Champs, a youth athletic program in inner cities. Wilma and other athletes visited urban neighborhoods in the nation's largest cities. They hoped to inspire young athletes whose worlds were filled with poverty and prejudice. Working in the ghettos, Wilma was reminded of her own upbringing in a rural, segregated southern town. She tackled the job with her usual enthusiasm, but she was greatly disturbed by the violence she saw.

The 1960s were a time of great turmoil in the United

States as blacks struggled to gain the rights to which they were entitled under the U.S. Constitution. Civil rights leaders such as Martin Luther King Jr. mobilized black Americans to protest social, political, and economic mistreatment, particularly in the South. In large cities, including the ones Wilma visited for Operation Champs, violent protests and riots erupted.

After Wilma completed her work with Operation Champs, she moved to St. Louis and then to Detroit, Michigan, where she taught again. "Eight years had gone by since I won the three gold medals in the Olympics, and I still hadn't found the fulfillment outside of track that I had found in it," Wilma said.

In the 1970s, Wilma decided to make a radical move to California. She found a job working in a community

Wilma with President Carter in 1979

Wilma, second from right, *and high school sweetheart Robert Eldridge,* far right, *relax at home with their children.*

center, but the old problems didn't go away. She was paid a small salary and was frustrated by her inability to get anything done. Her family grew—in 1971 she gave birth to her fourth child and second son, Xurry—and she needed a larger income to support them.

She moved her family to Chicago so she could work for the Mayor Daley Youth Foundation, but that job, too, proved frustrating. Wilma realized that many people were hiring her to capitalize on her fame. They wanted to be able to say that Wilma Rudolph worked for their organization, but they didn't want to give her any responsibility or the freedom to make changes. They weren't paying her very well, either.

"I knew that, since 1960, I had been a good wife and mother, but I was besieged with money problems; people were always expecting me to be a star, but I

wasn't making the money to live like one. I felt ex-
ploited both as a woman and as a black person." Ac-
companying the frustrations in her career were
difficulties in her marriage. She and Robert divorced
in 1976.

Wilma took her life in a completely new direction
then. Rather than seek employment, she founded her
own company, Wilma Unlimited. She wrote her autobiography, which was published in 1977, and served
as a consultant to movie producers who made her
book into a movie that same year. Later she founded
the Wilma Rudolph Foundation, a nonprofit community sports program in Indianapolis. She told young
athletes who benefited from the program, "You must
make sure your goals are your own, not someone
else's. Because no one can do it for you."

Taking charge of her own life, Wilma realized she
was in great demand. She spoke at events and even
found some work as a spokesperson for companies,
such as Minute Maid and Keebler. It took twenty
years for the commercial endorsements to be offered
to Wilma, but she kept a level head. She made sure
the products she endorsed would not tarnish her
image. "I'm selective because I am a legend," she said.

By breaking racial and gender barriers in the 1960s,
Wilma paved the way for new generations of female
runners to follow in her footsteps. "Wilma's accom-
plishments opened up the real door for women in
track and field, because of her grace and beauty," said

Nell Jackson, who had coached Wilma in the 1956 Olympics. "People saw her as beauty in motion."

Wilma had become a role model for a new generation of athletes. Florence Griffith Joyner and Jackie Joyner-Kersee were among those who looked up to Wilma. Even Wilma's oldest daughter, Yolanda, followed in her famous mother's footsteps, earning a scholarship to TSU in the 1970s and running briefly as a Tigerbelle. "She never developed the love for track that I had," Wilma said. "I think she would have if the press hadn't compared the two of us. That made it hard for her."

While running her foundation, Wilma continued to work in other positions. She became a public relations administrator for a bank, a vice president for a Tennessee hospital, a fashion model, a talk-show host, and a coach for DePauw University in Indiana. She also continued to travel for the foundation. When her children were still young and Wilma had to travel, they would stay with relatives while she was gone. "When she came home from a road trip, we rarely did anything special," Robert Jr. remembered. "Just seeing her was enough."

In 1984 Wilma was inducted into the Olympic Hall of Fame. Although she rarely ran for pleasure or fitness after retiring from track, Wilma stayed with the Olympics her entire life, promoting the Games and making television appearances. "The Olympics were a positive aspect of my life," Wilma said. "That one

Wilma's oldest daughter Yolanda, left, *earned a scholarship to TSU and ran briefly as a Tigerbelle. She's pictured with Wilma,* right.

accomplishment—what happened in 1960—nobody
can take from me. It was something I worked for. It
wasn't something somebody handed me."

Unfortunately, Wilma experienced financial difficulties for the rest of her life. In the 1990s, she had to
file for bankruptcy protection, and she had costly dis-
putes over her finances with the Internal Revenue Service. Despite these problems, Wilma continued to be
recognized for her contributions to athletics. In 1991
she joined Olympic champions Scott Hamilton, an ice-
skater, and Jeff Blatnick, a wrestler, in New York to
receive the Crown Royal Achievement Award for their
courage in overcoming physical ailments. In 1993
President Bill Clinton honored Wilma and four other
athletes at the first National Sports Awards.

Wilma's hometown continued to praise her as its
most-famous and most-loved citizen. In 1992 the
Clarksville town council named part of a highway running through town Wilma Rudolph Boulevard.

Wilma accepted the honors and accolades because
they allowed her to complete more important work—
inspiring others. "I have spent a lifetime trying to
share what it has meant to be a woman first in the
world of sports so that other young women have a
chance to reach their dreams," she said.

Wilma remained active in the Olympic organization after her retirement and always remembered the Rome Games with pride.

Chapter **TEN**

THE FINAL RACE

WHILE STRUGGLING FINANCIALLY IN THE **1990s,**
Wilma encountered an even bigger obstacle. In July
1994, the track legend was diagnosed with brain cancer after she became ill giving a speech in Atlanta,
Georgia. Wilma responded to the news with charac-
teristic spirit. Determined to beat the disease, she
spent the next five months in and out of the hospital
receiving painful cancer treatments. Despite doctors'
efforts, the cancer spread quickly throughout her
body. Wilma Rudolph died in her Nashville home on
November 14, 1994, at age fifty-four.

When Olympic medalist Evelyn Ashford heard the
news of Wilma's battle with cancer and her subse-
quent death, she was shocked. "The last time I saw

her, last year, she mentioned that her son was fighting cancer and that her mother was not feeling well," Ashford said in 1995. "She talked about her family. But she never mentioned any problems of her own. It wasn't her way."

Throughout her life, Wilma had been a role model and an inspiration. To those who grew up poor in the segregated South, she was proof that there was life beyond prejudice and poverty. Others took inspiration from Wilma's zeal for life and her dedication to success.

Upon Wilma's death, track star Florence Griffith Joyner said Wilma's life had been a blueprint for her

Wilma was an inspiration to track star Florence Griffith Joyner, left.

own success. "Whenever I was down, I often thought about how dedicated Wilma was to overcome the obstacles. That motivated me to push harder."

On the TSU campus, where Wilma had continued to interact with students long after her own track career had ended, students mourned the loss of a mentor and friend. "She'll be greatly missed on this campus," said Sonja Cliff, a TSU student in 1994. "She's part of its history, part of our history. She really influenced all of us."

Wilma's casket was on view at the TSU track stadium, and hundreds came to say a final farewell to the Tennessee Tornado. Nearly two thousand people attended Wilma's funeral in Clarksville's First Baptist Church, including the Burt High School Class of 1958 and former and current Tigerbelles. When all seats were taken, mourners filled the aisles and leaned against walls. Wilma's granddaughter, Wilma Whitlow, joined politicians, Olympic athletes, and celebrities in speaking at the service.

"In her passing, she is still giving and bringing Clarksville closer together," said Clarksville mayor Don Trotter. Those who remembered the 1960 homecoming parade that integrated Clarksville nodded in agreement, their hearts heavy with the memory.

Sportswriter Fred Russell, who had covered the 1960 Olympics, recalled for the crowd of mourners that day in 1960 when Wilma made Olympic history. "The day for me was—and still is—my top thrill in my sixty-six years of sportswriting," he told the crowd. "She was more than the fastest woman of her time. She was a symbol of courage, the personification of the idealism of the Olympic Games."

Wilma's old friend Mae Faggs, by then a retired teacher, remembered her friend fondly. "She was her family's champion, coach Ed Temple's, friends', but not the least the Tigerbelles' champion. We will miss her the rest of our lives."

Wilma was laid to rest in Clarksville, the Olympic flag draped across her coffin. After her death, her hometown came together to honor her, as it had done thirty-four years earlier when Wilma had returned from the Olympics a champion. Clarksville citizens organized the Wilma Memorial Fund Committee to raise funds for a statue of Wilma. Nearly six thousand people and twenty corporate sponsors donated money. In 1996 Wilma's hometown unveiled the bronze statue. Created by Clarksville artist Howard Brown, it depicts a youthful Wilma crossing a finish line. "This statue will remind everyone in the community to keep striving," Wilma's sister Charlene said during the dedication ceremony. "Wilma never gave up."

"This marks another finish line in the history of Wilma Rudolph," said Mayor Trotter. "This statue represents the spirit of Wilma Rudolph that is in all of us."

There were many other tributes to Wilma. In 1995, on the day that would have been Wilma's fifty-fifth birthday, Clarksville citizens organized the Wilma

Rudolph Birthday Breakfast to raise money for the Wilma Rudolph Track Scholarship, newly established at Austin Perry State University in Clarksville. The birthday breakfast endures and is held each year to raise additional funds for the scholarship. In 1997 Tennessee governor Don Sundquist proclaimed Wilma's birthday as Wilma Rudolph Day in the state that year. "Wilma will always be remembered for her inspirational determination to overcome her physical disabilities, always standing with her head high regardless of what problems may have been in her path," the governor said.

More enduring than the three gold medals Wilma brought home from the 1960 Olympic Games is the example she set through a life well lived. Forever an optimist, Wilma overcame obstacles of illness and poverty early in her life to achieve what few can even dream of. She inspired a generation of athletes with her strength, courage, and ability.

"It's been a roller-coaster life," she once told a reporter. "God has blessed me in many ways."

SOURCES

8   "Great Olympic Moments: Wilma Rudolph, Rome, 1960," *Ebony*, January 1992, 68.

9   Wilma Rudolph, *Wilma*, New York: New American Library, 1977, 13.

9   Ibid, 12.

12   Ibid, 7.

13   Ibid, 8.

13   Ibid.

13   Ibid.

13   Ibid, 16.

16   Michael D. Davis, *Black American Women in Olympic Track and Field*, Jefferson, North Carolina: McFarland & Company, Inc., Publishers, 1992, 111.

16   Ibid.

16   Rudolph, 19.

17   Ibid, 34.

17   Ibid, 30.

18   Ibid, 16.

18   "Wilma's Promise Good as Gold," The *San Diego Union-Tribune*, February 7, 1984, D1.

18   Marney Rich Keenan, "Wilma Rudolph," *Chicago Tribune*, January 8, 1989, C3.

18   Rudolph, 29.

19   Ibid, 37.

19   Susan Reed and Jane Sanderson, "Born to Win," *People Weekly*, November 28, 1994, 62–63.

19   Rudolph, 18.

19   Ibid, 22.

22   Ibid, 32.

23   Keenan, C3.

25   "World Speed Queen," *New York Times*, September 9, 1960, 20.

26   Keenan, C3.

26   Rudolph, 26.

27   Keenan, C3.

28   Ibid.

29   Ibid.

29 Rudolph, 43.
30 "World Speed Queen," 20.
30 Rudolph, 49.
31 Ibid, 62.
31 Ibid, 49.
31 Ibid, 55.
32 "Burt Runnerup in State Tournament; Girls 3rd," The *Leaf-Chronicle*, March 19, 1956.
32 "Burt Girls to Qualify for State Track," The *Leaf-Chronicle*, April 23, 1956.
33 Rudolph, 50.
36 Rudolph, 64.
36–37 Ibid.
40 Rudolph, 75-76.
40 Ibid, 78.
41 Ibid, 79.
44 Davis, 112.
45 Rudolph, 84.
45 Ibid.
46 Ibid, 85.
48 Ibid, 88.
48 Ibid, 90.
49 Ibid, 89.
53 Ibid, 97.
55 Keenan, C3.
57 Rudolph, 104.
58 Ibid, 101-102.
60 Ibid, 105.
61 Ibid, 107.
61 Ibid, 108.
61 Ibid.
62 Ibid, 12-13.
62 Ibid, 112.
63 Ibid, 111.
64 Ibid.
64 Ibid, 112.
64 Ibid, 111.
67 Ibid, 116.
70 Ibid, 121.

70   Ibid, 125.

71   Ibid, 128.

72   Ibid, 131.

72   *American Women of Achievement,* "Wilma Rudolph." Produced and directed by Wolfington Productions, Inc., and Schlessinger Productions, 1995. 30 min. Videocassette.

72   Rudolph, 135.

73   Ibid.

74   Ibid, 136.

75   *Wilma Rudolph,* Wolfington Productions, Inc., and Schlessinger Productions.

75   Cary B. Willis, "Sculptor Crafts Wilma Rudolph to Honor, Inspire," The *Courier-Journal,* April 7, 1996, 1B.

75   Lyn Votava, "Ahead of Their Time," *Runner's World,* June 1993, 51.

75   Rudolph, 136.

77   Ted Power, "1960: Wilma Charmed the World," The *Tennessean,* November 13, 1994, 18A.

77   Robert M. Lipsyte, "Wilma Rudolph Pauses Briefly for Medal, Visit and Plaudits," *New York Times,* September 27, 1960, 46.

77   Rudolph, 141.

80   Dan Coleman, "Clarksville Unrolls 'Carpet' for Wilma," The *Leaf-Chronicle,* October 5, 1960.

81   Ibid.

81   Rudolph, 145.

82   Ibid, 150.

82   Jim East and Tom Wood, "The Greatest Remembers a Champion," The *Tennessean,* November 13, 1994, 1.

82   Rudolph, 146.

83   Ibid, 147.

84   Ibid, 159.

85   Ibid, 152-153.

85   Ibid, 153.

85   Ibid.

88   Ibid, 155.

89   Ibid, 153.

90   Ibid, 161.

91–92   Ibid, 163.

92   Margaret Sheridan, "Even off the Track, Keeping Up with Olympian Wilma Rudolph Is No Mean Feat," *Chicago Tribune*, June 15, 1988, 18.

92   Gerald Eskenazi, "Scouting: Still on the Run," *New York Times*, October 8, 1982, B18.

92   William C. Rhoden, "Backtalk: Rudolph's Legacy, Triumph Over Pain," *New York Times*, June 20, 1993, Sports section, 9.

93   Ibid.

93   Ross Atkin, "Olympic Sprinter of 20 Years Ago Still Sprints—in the Business World," The *Christian Science Monitor*, July 31, 1980, 16.

93   "Growing Up with a Famous Mother: Children Tell of the Joy and Trials of Having a Distinguished Parent," *Ebony*, May 1989, 127.

93–94   "What Ever Happened to Wilma Rudolph?" *Ebony*, February 1984, 85-87.

95   Keenan, 3C.

97–98   Evelyn Ashford, "Lives Well Lived: Wilma Rudolph," *New York Times*, January 1, 1995, Section 6, 37.

99   "Florence Joyner Pays Tribute to the Late Wilma Rudolph," *Jet*, December 12, 1994, 51.

99   Jim East, "Students at TSU Remember Rudolph as Role Model, Hero," The *Tennessean*, November 13, 1994, 4A.

99   Marc Ira Hooks, "Olympic Athlete Honored," The *Leaf-Chronicle*, July 19, 1996, A1.

99–100   Karen Pulfer Focht, "Rest Well Wilma," The *Commercial Appeal*, November 19, 1994, A1.

100   "1,500 Attend Rudolph Service," *Chicago Tribune*, November 20, 1994.

100   Hooks, A1.

100–101   "Track Scholarship to Honor Wilma Rudolph," the City of Clarksville, Tennessee, Office of the Mayor/Public Affairs Office, June 14, 1998.

101   "Governor Proclaims June 23 as Wilma Rudolph Day," News release from the Office of the Governor of the State of Tennessee, June 20, 1997.

101   Turner, Miki. "Honoring Wilma: The Stand-Up Thing for a Nation to Do," *Orange County Register*, June 22, 1993, D2.

BIBLIOGRAPHY

BOOKS

Bureau of the Census. *Historical Statistics of the United States.* Washington, D.C.: U.S. Department of Congress, 1975.

Davis, Michael D. *Black American Women in Olympic Track and Field.* Jefferson, North Carolina: McFarland & Company, Inc., Publishers, 1992.

Laklaw, Carli. *Golden Girls: True Stories of Olympic Women Stars.* New York: McGraw Hill Book Company, 1980.

Rood, Karen L., *American Decades: 1940–1949.* Detroit: Gale Research, Inc., 1995.

Rudolph, Wilma. *Wilma.* New York: New American Library, 1977.

Smith, Jessie Carney, ed. *Epic Lives.* Detroit: Visible Ink Press, 1993.

Wollum, Janet. *Outstanding Women Athletes.* Phoenix: The Oryx Press, 1992.

World Book. Chicago: World Book, Inc., 1995.

MAGAZINES AND NEWSPAPER ARTICLES

"1,500 Attend Rudolph Service." *Chicago Tribune,* November 20, 1994.

Ashford, Evelyn. "Lives Well Lived: Wilma Rudolph." *New York Times,* January 1, 1995, section 6, p. 37.

Atkin, Ross. "Olympic Sprinter of 20 Years Ago Still Sprints—in the Business World." The *Christian Science Monitor,* July 31, 1980, p. 16.

"Burt Girls to Qualify for State Track." The *Leaf-Chronicle,* April 23, 1956.

"Burt Runnerup in State Tournament; Girls 3rd." The *Leaf-Chronicle,* March 19, 1956.

Coleman, Dan. "Clarksville Unrolls 'Carpet' for Wilma." The *Leaf-Chronicle,* October 5, 1960.

East, Jim. "Students at TSU Remember Rudolph as Role Model, Hero." The *Tennessean,* November 13, 1994, p. 4A.

East, Jim and Tom Wood. "The Greatest Remembers a Champion." The *Tennessean*, November 13, 1994, p. 1.

Eskenazi, Gerald. "Scouting: Still on the Run." *New York Times*, October 8, 1982, p. B18.

"Florence Joyner Pays Tribute to the Late Wilma Rudolph." *Jet*, December 12, 1994, p. 51.

Focht, Karen Pulfer. "Rest Well Wilma." The *Commercial Appeal*, November 19, 1994, p. A1.

"Great Olympic Moments: Wilma Rudolph, Rome, 1960." *Ebony*, January 1992, p. 68.

"Growing Up with a Famous Mother: Children Tell of the Joy and Trials of Having a Distinguished Parent." *Ebony*, May 1989, p. 127.

Hooks, Marc Ira. "Olympic Athlete Honored." The *Leaf-Chronicle*, July 19, 1996, p. A1.

Keenan, Marney Rich. "Wilma Rudolph." *Chicago Tribune*, January 8, 1989, p. C3.

Lewis, Dwight. "Rudolph Fights to Beat Cancer." The *Tennessean*, August 7, 1994, p. 1.

Lipsyte, Robert M. "Wilma Rudolph Pauses Briefly for Medal, Visit and Plaudits." *New York Times*, September 27, 1960, p. 46.

Power, Ted. "1960: Wilma Charmed the World." The *Tennessean*, November 13, 1994, p. 18A.

Reed, Susan and Jane Sanderson. "Born to Win." *People Weekly*, November 28, 1994, pp. 62-63.

Rhoden, William C. "Backtalk: Rudolph's Legacy, Triumph Over Pain." *New York Times*, June 20, 1993, Sports section, p. 9.

Sheridan, Margaret. "Even off the Track, Keeping Up with Olympian Wilma Rudolph Is No Mean Feat." *Chicago Tribune*, June 15, 1988, p. 18.

Votava, Lyn. "Ahead of Their Time." *Runner's World*, June 1993, p. 51.

"What Ever Happened to Wilma Rudolph?" *Ebony*, February 1984, pp. 85-87.

Willis, Cary B. "Sculptor Crafts Wilma Rudolph to Honor, Inspire." The *Courier-Journal*, April 7, 1996, p. 1B.

"Wilma Hopes to Justify Faith of Those Who Believe in Her." The *Leaf-Chronicle*, October 5, 1960, p. 1.

"Wilma's Promise Good as Gold." The *San Diego Union-Tribune*, February 7, 1984, p. D1.

"World Speed Queen." *New York Times*, September 9, 1960, p. 20.

NEWS RELEASES

"Governor Proclaims June 23 as Wilma Rudolph Day," the Office of the Governor of the State of Tennessee, Nashville, June 20, 1997.

"Track Scholarship to Honor Wilma Rudolph," the City of Clarksville, Tennessee, Office of the Mayor/Public Affairs Office, June 14, 1998.

RESOLUTIONS

"A Resolution designating the section of State Highway 13 (U.S. Highway 79) from such highway's intersection with Interstate 24 to the Red River as 'Wilma Rudolph Boulevard.'" (Resolution Number 84, 1991–1992), City of Clarksville, Tennessee, May 7, 1992.

VIDEO

American Women of Achievement, "Wilma Rudolph." Produced and directed by Wolfington Productions, Inc., and Schlessinger Productions, 1995. 30 min.

WEB SITE

Knowledge Adventure Encyclopedia, 1997. http://www.adventure.com/encyclopedia/america/bookert.html

FOR FURTHER READING

Biracree, Tom. *Wilma Rudolph: Champion Athlete.* New York: Chelsea House, 1988.

Krull, Kathleen. *Wilma Unlimited: How Wilma Rudolph Became the World's Fastest Woman.* New York: Harcourt Brace and Co., 1996.

Rudolph, Wilma. *Wilma.* New York: New American Library, 1977.

Sherrow, Victoria. *Wilma Rudolph.* Minneapolis, Minnesota: Carolrhoda Books, 1998.

Sherrow, Victoria. *Wilma Rudolph: Olympic Champion.* New York: Chelsea House Book Publishers, 1995.

INDEX

OTHER TITLES FROM LERNER AND A&E®:

Arthur Ashe
Bruce Lee
Christopher Reeve
George Lucas
Jesse Owens
Jesse Ventura
John Glenn
Legends of Dracula
Louisa May Alcott

Madeleine Albright
Maya Angelou
Mother Teresa
Nelson Mandela
Princess Diana
Queen Cleopatra
Rosie O'Donnell
Wilma Rudolph
Women in Space

ABOUT THE AUTHOR

Amy Ruth is a writer in Virginia, and she teaches college composition. She has a master's degree in journalism from the University of Iowa and writes regularly for magazines and newspapers. She and her writer/photographer husband, Jim Meisner, often collaborate on projects. This is her third book in the BIOGRAPHY® series.

PHOTO ACKNOWLEDGMENTS

Photographs are reproduced with the permission of: © AP/Wide World Photos, pp. 2, 14, 46, 53, 56, 66, 69, 76, 80, 83, 86, 91, 96; Courtesy of Clarksville-Montgomery County Museum, p. 6; © Library of Congress, p. 12; © UPI/Corbis-Bettmann, pp. 21, 42, 84, 88, 90, 94; © The Leaf Chronicle, p. 24; © Moorland-Spingarn Research Center, p. 28; © Photofest, p. 32; Courtesy of Charlene Rudolph, p. 34; © Brooklyn Dodgers, p. 41; © Archive Photos/Barnaby's, p. 51; © Popperfoto/Archive Photos, pp. 54, 78; © Joseph Roberts Collection/Clarksville-Montgomery County Public Schools, p. 59; Courtesy of Ed and Charlie B. Temple, p. 64; © Reuters/Nick Didlick/Archive Photos, p. 98.

Front and back covers: © UPI/Corbis-Bettmann.